THE HISTORY OF QUILTS AND PATCHWORK WORLDWIDE WITH PHOTOGRAPHIC REPRODUCTIONS

BY

SHIELA BETTERTON

British Library Cataloguing-in-Publication Data
A catalogue record for this book is available from the
British Library

Contents

Quilting

Quilting can refer either to the process of creating a quilt or to the sewing of two or more layers of material together to make a thicker padded material. 'Quilting' as the process of creating a quilt, refers specifically to the joining of layers as one of its steps, often along with designing, piecing, appliqué, binding and other stages. A quilter is the name given to someone who works at quilting. Quilting can be done by hand, by sewing machine, or by a specialist longarm quilting system.

The word 'quilt' comes from the Latin culcita meaning a 'large stuffed sack', but it came into the English language from the French word cuilte. The origins of quilting remain unknown, but sewing techniques of piecing, applique, and quilting have been used for clothing and furnishings in diverse parts of the world for several millennia. The earliest known quilted garment is depicted on the carved ivory figure of a Pharaoh of the Egyptian First Dynasty, about 3400 B.C.

Quilting has been part of the needlework tradition in Europe from about the 5th century CE. Early objects contain Egyptian cotton, which may indicate that Egyptian and Mediterranean trade provided a conduit for the technique. Quilted objects were relatively rare in Europe until approximately the twelfth century however, when quilted bedding and other items appeared after the return of the Crusaders from the Middle East. The medieval quilted gambeson, aketon and arming doublet were garments worn under, or instead of, armour of maille or plate armour. These developed into the later quilted doublet worn as part of fashionable European male clothing from the fourteenth to the seventeenth century. Quilting clothing began to be generally used in the fourteenth century, with quilted doublets and armour worn in France, Germany, and England and quilted tunics in Italy.

Typical quilting is done with three layers: the top fabric or quilt top, batting or insulating material and backing material. The quilter's hand or sewing machine passes the needle and thread through all layers and then brings the needle back up. This process is repeated across the entire area where quilting is wanted. A rocking, straight or running stitch is commonly used and these stitches can be purely functional or decorative and elaborate. Likewise, the usage of the finished quilts can be purely for artistic purposes, or for more functional reasons; items such as bed spreads, clothing and various textile products.

Many types of quilting exist today. The two most widely used are hand-quilting and machine quilting; Machine quilting is the process of using a home sewing machine or a longarm machine to sew the layers together. With the home sewing machine, the layers are tacked together before quilting. This involves laying the top, batting, and backing out on a flat surface and either pinning (using large safety pins) or tacking the layers together. Longarm Quilting involves placing the layers to be quilted on a special frame. The frame has bars on which the layers are rolled, keeping these together without the need for tacking or pinning. A longarm machine is moved across the fabric, but in contrast, with a home sewing machine, the fabric is moved through it.

Hand quilting is the process of using a needle and thread to sew a running stitch, by hand, across the entire area to be quilted. This binds the layers together. A quilting frame or hoop is often used to assist in holding the piece being quilted off the quilter's lap. A quilter can make one stitch at a time by first driving the needle through the fabric from the right side, then pushing it back up through the material from the wrong side to complete the stitch; this is called a stab stitch. Another option is called a rocking stitch, where the quilter has one hand, usually with a finger wearing a thimble, on top of the quilt, while the other hand is located beneath the piece to push the needle back up. A third option is called 'loading the needle' and involves doing four or more stitches before pulling the needle through the cloth. The process of hand quilting is currently experiencing a resurgence worldwide, especially with the growing popularity of various homecrafts. We hope that the reader is inspired by this book to try some quilting of their own. Enjoy.

QUILTING AND PATCHWORK - WORLD-WIDE NEEDLE ARTS

By Shiela Betterton

It may come as a surprise to many to realise that quilting and patchwork have been known for such a long time, particularly as patchwork, or pieced work as it is often known, has come to be regarded as something peculiarly American. However, study and research have shown that these two forms of needlework are to be found in countries as far apart as Britain and Australia, India and North America, and there are few countries in the world where these crafts cannot be found in one form or another.

The true quilt is atextile sandwich, with a top layer, a bottom layer and a filling in the middle. Quilting is the pattern in running stitch which holds the three layers together and is the last process in the making of a quilt. A quilt top may be of whole cloth, pieced work or appliqué or a combination of them all. In Britain a quilter is one who quilts only, but in the United States of American the term "quilter" is used for those who make patchwork whether it is quilted or not.

In Britain and Europe patchwork and quilting are two very different forms of needlework. Both come from the east, spread through the middle east and North Africa to Europe, to Britain and eventually to North America.

Some of the earliest patchwork in existence today was made between the 6th and 9th centuries. It is of a type now known as mosaic patchwork and the pieces have been whipped together on the wrong side in the English manner. The work formed part of votive offerings in a temple on one of the silk routes between China and India. It is interesting to note that this work would probably have been done by a man as women were not usually allowed in temples.[1]

Quilting too came from the east. Quilted jackets have been worn by the Chinese people for many hundreds of years. During the Crusades, and later, men wore quilted jackets under their heavy metal armour in order to be more comfortable. For light troops a quilted jacket was the only protection. When soldiers first came to Jamestown in 1607 they wore padded jackets in place of armour.

Early quilts were purely utilitarian, just a stuffed sack (the word quilt is derived from the Latin "culcita" meaning a stuffed mattress or cushion). The three layers were tied together at intervals just sufficient to prevent the padding from moving. Gradually fine stitching and elaborate patterns evolved. Houses were cold, glass for windows unknown and thick warm bedcovers and bed hangings were essential.

The reasons for patchwork were obviously repair and economy. When textiles were scarce, pieces left over from rich clothing or the best pieces left when church vestments had worn out were applied to another background to make a new piece of cloth. The appliqués took the place of embroidery. The original coat-of-arms was actually a jacket with shapes appliquéd to it.2

During the eighteenth century quilted clothing was high fashion. Men wore quilted breeches and quilted waistcoats (vests), women wore quilted bodices and lovely quilted petticoats. Many of these were made of silk with a homespun backing and a sheeps wool filling, but some were made of a fine worsted fabric called calamanco. Fashions in clothing crossed the Atlantic and women in the American colonies would be wearing the same fashionable clothes as were being worn in London, within a very short time.

Before the War of Independence British and American best quilts were very similar, often made of calamanco which was imported into America from England with the sheep's wool filling. The traditional North of England and Welsh quilts were, and still are, whole cloth, usually in solid colours, white or pastels, with perhaps one colour for the top and a contrast for the back. Contrary to the opinion expressed in many American books, British quilts are always quilted in running stitch, not back stitch. Running stitch means that the quilt can be completely reversible.

Quilting skills were taken out to America from Europe but there is no mention in contemporary literature of patchwork as we know it today. Early patchwork would have been literally "patched" work where a patch would have been applied to a threadbare spot. The main quilting areas in Britain are in the north of England and south Wales, and the quilting patterns are regional. Those from the north are free and flowing and all the feather patterns come from this area - patterns called in the United States of America the Princess Feathers. The pattern layouts from Wales are inclined to be more geometric. Of course when women emigrated to North America they took their quilting patterns with them, and as they journeyed throughout the north American continent so the patterns spread. Similar patterns are used for both quilting, appliqué and patchwork, and the meanings are the same. For instance the pineapple is the symbol of hospitality, the pomegranate fruitfulness, the vine plenty and so on.

It was usual in Britain for a girl to have just one quilt for her dowry but in America, tradition has it that a girl should have twelve or even thirteen, the thirteenth being the grandest one of all, her Bride's Quilt. Factory-made blankets were not readily available until after the Civil War. Cold winters and unheated homes meant that young women would need a goodly store of quilts, even if not as many as thirteen, before marriage as there would not be too much time for making quilts in the early years after marriage. The continuing westward expansion meant that there was always a need for warm bedding, and throughout the years women continued to meet the challenge of finding new ways of piecing together their scraps of fabric, old and new, found in the family scrap bag. By the middle of the nineteenth century designing quilt block patterns had become one of the most popular domestic pastimes. It is not known exactly when, in America, the block method of construction superseded the whole cloth quilt. No doubt there was a transitional period when both types were being made simultaneously. The straight lines of the geometric patterns were easy to sew, and pieces could be cut economically.

Leisure meant time for sewing and distances between the homes of many of the pioneer women meant that they had to concentrate on occupations and hobbies which could be carried on in the home. Quilting bees were welcome social occasions where the whole family could join in. The women sewed and provided a grand supper. After work was over for the day the men joined in the festivities which often included dancing and social activities. The young people particularly enjoyed these occasions as it gave them a chance to meet others of their own age and perhaps do a little courting. In Britain, as in America, quilting served many purposes. Many a church or chapel has been built or repaired from the proceeds of quilting bees, and women in both countries have kept the family together by quilting for a living when times were hard.

However many more quilts must have been made at home than ever were made at quilting parties, and a quilting frame was an essential piece of furniture. Types of frame varied from the simple "stretcher" type which could be rested on the backs of two chairs for support, to a full-sized frame which was pulled up to the ceiling when quilting was over for the day. Similar types of frames to those used in America were used in northern England and Wales.

Quilting in Britain persisted in country districts and particularly in the mining areas of south Wales and the northeast of England. In these areas the fashion for wearing quilted petticoats lasted well into the twentieth century. Many Welsh women owned a black satin quilted petticoat, and on the northeast coast fisherwomen wore heavy woollen petticoats with a thick rib quilted horizontally. Others wore the more traditional type of quilted petticoat.

The north of England produced a type of quilt which was not made elsewhere. Called "Strippy" quilt, it consisted of seven or nine bands of fabric sewn together down the length of the quilt. Pieced or patterned fabric bands alternated with solid colour bands and the whole was skilfully quilted in traditional patterns. Did the Amish copy the idea for their "Bars" quilts or did the idea emerge simultaneously on both sides of the Atlantic?

During the last quarter of the 19th century Victorian "crazy" patchwork reached its peak. Silks, velvets, brocades and ribbons were all sewn together in seemingly careless abandon. The seams were heavily embellished with embroidery stitches and women vied with each other to see how elaborately they could sew. These ornate pieces of needlework were seldom used on beds, but were rather "throws" to be used on a sofa when resting. Many pieces of this work are still in existence, often in private homes, treasured pieces handed down in the family.

One pattern which seems to be common to all countries is that known as the "Log Cabin." In many parts of the north of England the pattern is known as "Log Wood" while in the Isle of Man it is known as "Roof" patterns and is considered to be "the true Manx pattern."3 In Ireland a Log Cabin quilt is called a "folded" quilt while Averil Colby mentions in her book *Patchwork* that a woman in Scotland possesses a number of quilts made by her family from patterns which had been handed down to them from the 18th century, some of which were "Log Cabin" made of tweed and homespun woollen cloth. Because ribbons were often used for the narrow "logs", Caulfeild's *Dictionary of Needlework* calls the pattern "ribbon patchwork."

In America the central square of the block traditionally is red, representing the fire. The light side of the block represents the firelight and the dark side the shadow. Sometimes the centre square is yellow which signifies the lantern put in the window to guide travellers. However there is no such symbolism in Britain. This pattern has been used to great effect in Holland but there the influence is directly from America.

Patchwork and quilting have often been undertaken by men. One of the first quilters to receive recognition was Joseph Hedley who lived near Hexham in Northumberland. Known as Joe the Quilter he became famous for his beautiful designs and exquisite stitchery. Unhappily for him in 1826 he was found cruelly beaten to death, some say for the wealth he had made by his quilting, but his murderers were never found.

During the 19th Century several men were known to have pieced coverlets from scraps of woolen cloths which were used to make military uniforms. In Wales, James Williams, a tailor of Wrexham, Denbighshire, spent ten years making a large coverlet from approximately 4,500 pieces of cloth left over from the garments he had made. This is now in the Welsh Folk Museum at St. Fagans, Cardiff. More recently, Mr. Rowley of Oxfordshire pieced coverlets (they were not quilted). He used fabrics given to him by the ladies of his village so that the coverlets were a record of all the dresses which they had worn.

There are many different types of quilts and quilts were made by many different types of people. Early in the 19th century textile manufacturers printed panels which commemorated some special event. These were often incorporated as the centre panel of a "medallion" or "framed" quilt. Queen Victoria's Jubilee in 1887 produced a great number of these prints as did the Centennial in 1876. Many Album quilts were made. They honoured someone, and each block would be executed by a different person or group of people and be signed and dated. The finished article would be presented to the recipient to mark some special occasion. One in the Museum's collection has inscribed in indelible ink "Presented to the Rev. Mrs. Waterbury by her friends on April 1st, 1853." Weldon's "Practical Patchwork" published about 1900 explains that "Hospital quilts are made of good-sized squares of red twill and white calico placed alternately like squares on a chess board, the white pieces having texts written on them or Scripture pictures outlined in marking ink; they are much appreciated and prove a great source of interest to the poor invalids."

Needlework skills have been acquired by many women who had no tradition of sewing with needle and thread, and the quilts made in Hawaii and by the Plains Indian women show that a very high standard of work has been attained.

Patterns did not always go from east to west. Most countries have records which show the influence of American patchwork on their own designs. A quilt made in the north of England in 1840 and used by the maker to pay her rent, shows a pattern of rather flamboyant tulip-like flowers. The maker's sister had emigrated to Philadelphia and was known

17

to have sent back patterns to her family in England. A large pieced top which had never been backed or quilted was made in Ireland in 1860, and is now in the possession of the Cheltenham Museum. It shows considerable Pennsylvania influence — blocks resembling hex signs, hearts and two love birds. The Ulster Folk and Transport Museum has set a set of six quilts made by one woman, some sewn in Co. Antrim and some in San Francisco, but it is impossible to tell which quilts were made in which country. Once again we see the interweaving of ideas between Britain and North America.

Contemporary literature mirrors the interests of the day and throughout the centuries references to quilting and patchwork abound. Quilts were mentioned in the fifteenth century and a quilted "cappe" in the sixteenth. In 1666 John Smith, clothier of Bradford on Avon, England left in his will, "one green rug, one pair of blancotts and one red coverlid." It was not specified whether the coverlet was quilted. But in 1726 William Trent of New Jersey had "feather beds, bolsters, blankets, ruggs and quoits to the value of £38.9s"

References to patchwork can be found in 18th century literature. In *Gulliver's Travels*, published in 1726 he states that his clothes, measured and fitted by three hundred Lilliputian tailors, "looked like the patchwork made by the ladies in England, only that mine were all of a colour."[4] Patchwork is mentioned in many nineteenth-century works such as *Oliver Twist* by Dickens and in most of the American and Canadian girls' stories. Books such as these provide valuable references to the type of patterns then in use.

During the summer of 1882 the writer, Oscar Wilde, held meetings in the U.S.A. He talked to select circles of women each of whom was busy embroidering and stitching an "Oscar" Crazy Quilt, the season's rage, thus described by an expert: "Or a piece of cambric half a yard square there is basted in the centre a sunflower made of either yellow broadcloth, silk or velvet; or else a lily, daisy or pansy. The squares are filled with bits of silk or velvet of all colours, the edges turned in, and the pieces sewed down firmly with a chain stitch of old gold colour, alternating with cardinal sewing silk."[5]

One of Scotland's oldest homes is Traquair House in Peebleshire. The family were Jacobite and faithful to the Young Pretender, Charles Stewart. As it was then an offence to practice the Catholic religion, services were held in secrecy in the house. The priest's vestments, which were white and quilted, were folded and placed among the piles of household linen and were thus quite unnoticed when not in use.

Legend has it that a white satin quilt on the bed in the King's Room at Traquair was made by Mary, Queen of Scots and her four Maries, but it has been established that the quilt is of a slightly later date. It is highly probable that Mary learnt to quilt when she lived in France but there is no record of any quilting actually executed by her. However, when she was imprisoned it was recorded that her steward sent her a "Holland cloak and a quilted bodice."[6]

It is thought that the English gentry introduced patchwork and quilting into Ireland during the 18th century, and these crafts spread through all classes of society. Strangely enough it was often the upper classes, who had no need of economy, who saved the best pieces from worn-out textiles for re-use, whereas the poorer people bought bundles of cloth pieces from the dressmaker or later the factory, for a very small sum of money. Was this because their clothes and household textiles were so worn that they could not be re-used? However, although thrift was a primary concern, even these quiltmakers designed their own patterns.

Most early work was chintz appliqué, often known in America as *Broderie Perse*. This was a process where motifs were cut from chintz, perhaps worn-out bedcovers or curtains, which were then sewn to a calico background thus making a new piece of patterned cloth. Most of the early Irish appliqués were sewn down with buttonhole stitch whereas in America the raw edge was turned under with the needle and neatly hemmed.

For piecing the Irish invariably used the American method whereby the geometric shapes of fabric were octagonal and sewn with a running stitch. Many of the hexagonal patterns were made by the English method, in which the cloth was basted over paper shapes which were then oversewn or whipped together on the wrong side. In Ireland it was quite usual to have best quilts and "using quilts".

The upper class ladies encouraged plain sewing and the making of patchwork among the less well-off. These were taught in the schools set up by landlords for the children of their tenants.

By the middle of the nineteenth century a good turkey red dye had become readily available, and like her sisters in Wales, northern England and the Isle of Man, the Irish needlewoman incorporated red-dyed fabric into many bedcovers. It looked well with white, and a plentiful supply of white fabric was always available, and it gave the illusion of warmth and cheer.

The quilting was kept very simple, - diamonds, squares or zig-zags, known as "wave" quilting. Most Irish quilts are just two layers, the batting being omitted.

The fashion for the Victorian crazy patchwork was short lived in Ireland, perhapes because there was not the wealth of rich fabrics available.

In northern Ireland, Ulster, women generally were thrifty and loved bright colours, so patchwork made a great appeal to them. Nearly all Ulster quilts have patchwork or appliqué tops and use one quilting pattern over the whole surface. As in southern Ireland the pattern is known as

"Waves" and resembles chevrons. These quilts seldom were padded but if padding was used it could have been old blankets, neatly cut up.

Quilting was a winter pastime and involved the whole community. The quilting parties held in Ulster very much resembled those of the United States of America. A woman who had a top ready for quilting sent out invitations and prepared as fine a supper as she could afford. The guests, men and women, started arriving in the late afternoon and as the women sewed in teams of six there was time for those not actually quilting to join in the general festivities. Young people particularly enjoyed these parties.

The Isle of Man, which is situated in the Irish Sea between the north-west coast of England and northern Ireland, had a strong tradition of patchwork. The Manx were a practical people and thought patchwork was an appropriate occupation for even the well-to-do. Such families could afford to buy materials from the mainland, England, to make quilts and had the time to piece blocks.

The main characteristic of Manx patchwork is the square used as a diamond and the more typical Manx quilts had larger blocks than was usual elsewhere. Suitings, flannels and tweeds were used as well as cottons, and the interlining was often worn blankets. Quilting was quick and simple just zig zag lines, known, as in Ireland, as the "wave" pattern. Whereas in England and Wales a quilting frame was always used, this was not the case in the Isle of Man, although itinerant quilters would travel from house to house carrying a portable quilting frame with them. "Flowers" of hexagons were often arranged in the manner of the American "Grandmother's Flower Garden" pattern but the most usual form was the framed quilt. A central panel, which was sometimes specially printed for the purpose, was surrounded by a number of borders either pieced or with solid colour borders alternating with pieced borders. These were sewn on until the required size had been reached.

Many quilts were made from bands of woollen cloth in the manner of the well-known Amish quilts. Immigrants from the Isle of Man settled in Ohio and other parts of the mid-West. Could it be that the Amish in the mid-west adopted the Manx idea for their "Bars" quilts?

A favourite pattern in American is known as the "Ohio Star." A block in this pattern was made at a school in Castletown, Isle of Man, about 1840. Cleveland, Ohio, was largely settled by people of Manx origin7 so again the intriguing question arises - Was this pattern taken from the Isle of Man to Cleveland, Ohio, where it became the "Ohio Star."

As in the north of England the women of the Isle of Man wore quilted skirts and quilted hoods even into the 20th century.

It has been recorded by Dr. Larch Garrard of the Isle of Man and Manx Museum that the cutting of patches, and the rag strips for the hooked rugs was the task of the daughters of the household, particularly of strict non-conformists, on summer evenings before they were allowed to go out. The use of patchwork quilts was widespread in the 19th and early 20th centuries, and during the nineteenth century all boarding houses in Douglas, the principal town of the island and a popular holiday resort, furnished their bedrooms with a "patchwork coverlet on every bed and a rag rug on every floor."[8]

Further afield in Holland, early Indian palampores (printed or painted bedcovers) were padded and quilted, and one in the Ryksmuseum is quilted in the clam-shell pattern. This pattern, of great antiquity (it was used at Pompeii) is not often seen on quilted or patchwork bedcovers. Another palampore which bears the arms of the City of Amsterdam is quilted overall in a Log Cabin pattern.

During the 19th century Dutch quilts were made of hexagons and many of the log cabin pattern. It is not known whether these particular patterns were used simultaneously in Holland and America or whether they show the influence of Dutch citizens on their return from the United States of America.

The nobility in Sweden slept under quilted silk bedcovers in the 17th century. As in the early Dutch quilts the clam-shell pattern was used, often as an all-over design. This same use can be found in quilts made in the north of England. These silk quilts had very little padding so it is presumed they were used as bedspreads only. Therefore a pile rug or "rya" was put on top for warmth.9 Here we come across another similarity between Europe and America, where in Connecticut, for approximately one hundred years (1722-1833) needlework bed rugs were used as the top cover of the bed.

The early 17th and 18th-century quilts were all made of silk but by the 19th century cotton, wool and silk were all commonly used. During the 18th and 19th centuries thicker wadding became more common and the quilts served a more practical function.

As time went on quilted bedcovers became common to most classes of people, and during the second half of the 19th century some patchwork was known to have been made by Swedes who had returned from America, showing the influence of the American block system of working.

Quilting skills from the Far East spread over most of Asia where men carried on the trade of quilters. In Persia prayer mats were quilted and even today it is possible to buy modern examples. In India and Pakistan, as in China itself, garments were quilted either overall or perhaps just around the bottoms of sleeves and trouser legs. In 1710 Celia Fiennes wrote in her diary "the next room has such a bed but that is fine Indian quilting." However, no explanation is given as to the type of quilting this could have been.

At the other side of the globe in Australia, Tasmania and New Zealand there is some tradition of quilting, no doubt derived from the skills taken out by British settlers. Elizabeth Fry the, great Quaker reformer, and her ladies taught patchwork to women prisoners in London's Newgate Goal while they were awaiting deportation to Australia. She believed in cheerful community work. Each woman was given a bag of pieces to sew together on her long journey to the Antipodes and she would be hopeful to sell her work when she landed thus earning a little money to start her new life there.[10]

The padding of Tasmanian quilts is not always, as one would expect in a wool-producing country, sheep's wool, but layers of cloth, similar to the padding used by the Chinese.

In America patchwork developed often to the detriment of quilting which was reduced to straight lines and the outlining of geometric shapes. In England and Wales, quilting was the first consideration, but sadly the art has almost died out. However, during the last few years patchwork has become increasingly popular and a few of the old time quilters are passing on their skills to younger women. Quilting groups are being farmed on the lines of many in America. If American women did not invent patchwork, they certainly developed it to an art which other countries have not yet been able to surpass. It is encouraging to hear of the many groups meeting regularly perpetuating the old skills and experimenting with new.

1 Patchwork, A. Colby

2 Patchwork, A. Colby

3 Dr. Larch Garrard

4 Patchwork, A. Colby

5 The Life of Oscar Wilde by Hesketh Pearson, Methuen 1946

6 The Needlework of Mary, Queen of Scots, by Margaret Swain

7 Dr. Larch Garrard

8 Dr. Larch Garrard

9 Nordiska Museet

10 Life of Elizabeth Fry, Janet Whitney.

Patchwork, A. Colby

1. WHOLE CLOTH QUILT. TOP OF INDIGO DYED
CALAMANCO, NATURAL HOMESPUN BACKING
WITH SHEEP'S WOOL FILLING.
American. Third quarter 18th C.

American Museum in Britain.

2. WHOLE CLOTH QUILT. STRIPED SILK IN PALE COLOURS.
Swedish. Late 18th C.

Nordiska Museet, Stockholm.

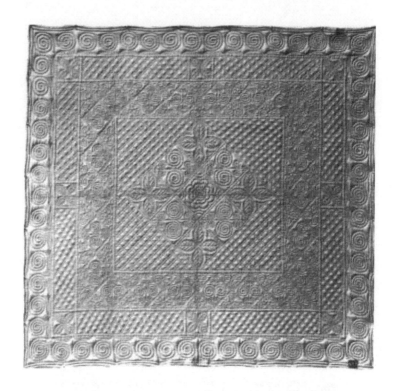

3. WHOLE CLOTH QUILT OF CREAM SILK POPLIN SHIRTING, WOOL FILLING. THE QUILTING IS A GEOMETRIC DESIGN OF GREAT INTRICACY IN-CORPORATING MANY TRADITIONAL WELSH PAT-TERNS.
Welsh. Made in 1952 by Miss Edwards of Glamorgan.

Welsh National Folk Museum, St. Fagans.

In the 1920's Miss Edwards had been taught the traditional patterns of the Glamorganshire valleys. In the 1930's she was one of the people appointed to be one of the official instructors to groups of miners' wives throughout the county thus instigating a revival of quilting. It was partly a "home industry" and partly social therapy for the wives during the difficult years of the depression.

4. FEATHER QUILT. RED AND GREEN APPLIQUÉ FEATHERS ON WHITE GROUND. INTRICATE QUILTING.
American. 19th C.

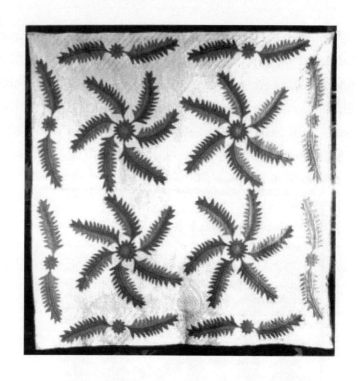

5. *FEATHER QUILT. PINK AND GREEN APPLIQUÉ FEATHERS AND TREE EVERLASTING BORDERS IN WHITE. BORDERS QUILTED IN WINEGLASS AND ROSE PATTERNS; OUTER BORDER FEATHER QUILT- ED.*

English. c1860. Made by the owner's great-grandmother in the Woodburn area of Northumberland, Mrs. J. Jackson.

6. PINEAPPLE QUILT. ORANGE PINEAPPLES AND GREEN FOLIAGE APPLIED TO WHITE COTTON. GREEN SWAGS AND ORANGE BOWS. COTTON FILL-ING WITH SEEDS LEFT IN.
American c1850. Made by Leila Adams Weston, possibly in Pennsylvania.

American Museum in Britain.

*7. TULIPS AND RIBBONS QUILT. YELLOW AND
RED TULIPS WITH GREEN RIBBONS APPLIED TO
WHITE COTTON. THE VIVID COLOURS ARE TYPI-
CAL OF THOSE USED FOR PENNSYLVANIA GERMAN
QUILTS.*
American 1840/50. Pennsylvania.

American Museum in Britain.

8. TULIP QUILT. RED AND ORANGE TULIPS OF A MORE FLAMBOYANT TYPE DECORATE THE TOP OF THE QUILT MADE BY PHOEBE WATSON OF IRE-SHOPEBURN, CO. DURHAM, ABOUT 1840.
English

Mrs. F. Milburn.

Miss Watson was a tenant of the owner's grandparents and was so poor that at times she was unable to pay her very modest rent. On one occasion she asked if this quilt could be taken in lieu of money. It was made by the light of a tallow candle. Phoebe Watson's sister Phyllis had emigrated to America and from time to time sent back patterns to her sister.

9. YORKSHIRE STAR QUILT. PIECED OF RED AND WHITE COTTONS. CABLE QUILTED.
English, ca.1860.

Mrs. I. Keighley.

10. CRAZY "THROW" MADE OF A WIDE VARIETY OF
SILKS, VELVETS AND BROCADES. THE BORDER IS
PALE GREY SILK AND PLUM VELVET.
American. Last quarter 19th C.

American Museum in Britain.

The donor's grandfather was a Federal Judge at Forth Leavenworth, Kansas. On his business trips to Baltimore he would buy silks and other dress fabrics for his wife and daughters and this throw was made from the scraps left over.

11. LOG CABIN QUILT.
Dutch. ca.1860

Het Nederlands Openluchtmuseum, Arnheim.

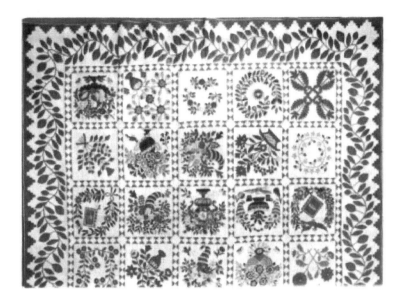

12. BALTIMORE BRIDE'S QUILT.

A very large quilt (122 inches square) of a type which was especially popular in the Baltimore area between 1842 and 1852. The hearts are geometric. A number of the blocks have been signed and one bears the signature "Alice A. Ryder, April 1st, 1847, Baltimore, Md."

American Museum in Britain.

14562644R00025

Printed in Great Britain
by Amazon.co.uk, Ltd.,
Marston Gate.